SPACE
CRUSADERS

Buzz Aldrin

Pioneer Moon Explorer

Jessie Alkire

Checkerboard
Library

An Imprint of Abdo Publishing
abdobooks.com

ABDOBOOKS.COM

Published by Abdo Publishing, a division of ABDO, PO Box 398166, Minneapolis, Minnesota 55439.
Copyright © 2019 by Abdo Consulting Group, Inc. International copyrights reserved in all countries.
No part of this book may be reproduced in any form without written permission from the publisher.
Checkerboard Library™ is a trademark and logo of Abdo Publishing.

Printed in the United States of America, North Mankato, Minnesota
102018
012019

Design: Kelly Doudna, Mighty Media, Inc.
Production: Mighty Media, Inc.
Editor: Liz Salzmann
Front Cover Photographs: NASA (both)
Back Cover Photographs: NASA (Aldrin, ISS, space shuttle, Apollo rocket), Shutterstock (planets)
Interior Photographs: AP Images, pp. 7, 23, 27, 29 (bottom); Getty Images, p. 13; NASA, pp. 5, 14, 15, 17, 19,
20, 21 (top left, top right, bottom left, bottom right), 28 (top right, bottom), 29 (top); Shutterstock, p. 25;
Wikimedia Commons, p. 11; Yearbook Library, pp. 9, 28 (top left)

Library of Congress Control Number: 2018948527

Publisher's Cataloging-in-Publication Data
Names: Alkire, Jessie, author.
Title: Buzz Aldrin: pioneer Moon explorer / by Jessie Alkire.
Other title: Pioneer Moon explorer
Description: Minneapolis, Minnesota : Abdo Publishing, 2019 | Series: Space
    crusaders | Includes online resources and index.
Identifiers: ISBN 9781532117015 (lib. bdg.) | ISBN 9781532159855 (ebook)
Subjects: LCSH: Aldrin, Buzz (Edwin Eugene Aldrin Jr.)--Juvenile literature. |
    Astronauts--United States--Biography--Juvenile literature. | Moon--
    Exploration--Juvenile literature. | Apollo 11 (Spacecraft)--Juvenile literature.
Classification: DDC 629.450 [B]--dc23

Contents

Footprints on the Moon

Buzz Aldrin is one of the best-known American astronauts. He was the second person to set foot on the moon! Aldrin was also a member of the US Air Force (USAF) and a pioneer in spacecraft **rendezvous** methods.

Aldrin was in the third group of astronauts **NASA** selected. During his career at NASA, he spent 289 hours and 53 minutes in space. He helped develop methods of working outside spacecraft while in space.

After his time at NASA, Aldrin struggled with **depression** and **alcoholism**. However, he turned his life around and has become a famous public figure. He has written several books, including **memoirs**, science fiction novels, and children's books.

Today, Aldrin is a supporter of building a human settlement on Mars. He has even patented plans for a spacecraft called the *Aldrin Mars Cycler*. This spacecraft could be used in the future for travel to Mars. No matter where Aldrin goes in the future, his footprints will always remain on the moon!

Born to Fly

Edwin Eugene Aldrin Jr. was born on January 20, 1930, in Montclair, New Jersey. He grew up there with his parents, Edwin Sr. and Marion, and two older sisters, Fay Ann and Maddy.

Edwin went by the nickname "Buzz." He got this name from his sister Fay Ann. She pronounced *brother* as "buzzer." Buzz's family shortened the name to Buzz.

Buzz's early life was shaped by his parents and their ties to the US military. His father was a colonel in the USAF. His mother's father was a **chaplain** in the US Army Air Corps.

Buzz became interested in **aviation** at an early age. He went on his first flight at the age of two. He flew in a small plane piloted by his father. The plane was called the *Eagle*. This was the same name as the spacecraft Buzz landed on the moon many years later. Buzz loved his first plane ride and couldn't wait to fly again.

STELLAR!
In 1988, Aldrin legally changed his first name to Buzz.

As an adult, Aldrin (*left*) had a troubled relationship
with his father, Edwin Sr. (*right*).

3 Military Education

Buzz continued to be interested in **aviation** throughout his youth. He also loved to play sports, including football. But eventually he stopped playing football to focus on school. Buzz also became interested in serving his country like his father had.

Buzz graduated from Montclair High School in 1947. He decided to join the military and attend the United States Military Academy in West Point, New York. This college is commonly known as West Point.

Aldrin did well as a **cadet** at West Point. He enjoyed the high standards that the cadets were held to. West Point also had an honor code. Buzz felt this code helped him develop **integrity** and accountability. In 1951, Buzz graduated third in his class.

Around this time, Aldrin met Joan Archer. Joan was a drama student at Rutgers University in New Jersey. The couple's parents had set them up on a date. As Aldrin and Joan's romance was getting started, Aldrin joined the USAF.

STELLAR!

West Point was President George Washington's headquarters during the **American Revolution**. The Military Academy was founded there in 1802.

8

Buzz worked hard in high school and graduated a year early.

Serving His Country

Aldrin's interest in **aviation** had made joining the USAF an easy choice. Aldrin trained as a fighter pilot and became qualified to fly the Sabre F-86 jet. The USAF had been using the Sabre F-86 since 1949. It was the main fighter jet used by the US during the **Korean War**.

In December 1952, Aldrin was sent to combat duty in the Korean War. Aldrin has recalled his duty in Korea as one of the most exciting times of his life. He and the other fighter pilots flew jets to protect South Korea from enemy forces in North Korea. During his duty, Aldrin flew 66 missions and shot down two enemy jets.

The war taught Aldrin about friendship and teamwork. On the missions, there was nothing more important than protecting his fellow servicemen. The Korean War ended in 1953. That year Aldrin returned to the United States to continue his USAF training.

STELLAR!
Aldrin served in the USAF from 1951 to 1972 and achieved the rank of colonel.

Aldrin received the Distinguished Flying Cross
for his service in the Korean War.

Journey to NASA

While training with the USAF, Aldrin continued to date Joan. The two married in December 1954. In 1955, their first child, Mike, was born. The couple had two more children, Jan and Andy, over the next four years. The family moved around frequently because of Aldrin's military duties.

In the late 1950s, Aldrin began working toward a new goal. He had heard about the United States' space program from a fellow fighter pilot, Ed White. Aldrin was excited about the possibility of going to space. But, he knew he needed to improve his math and science education. So, Aldrin started graduate school at the Massachusetts Institute of **Technology** (MIT). He received a **PhD** in **astronautics** in 1963.

Aldrin's PhD thesis was on space **rendezvous** concepts. A space rendezvous is when two spacecraft join together in space. **NASA** used Aldrin's docking and rendezvous methods in the Gemini and Apollo space programs. These methods are still used in space exploration today.

STELLAR!

The first group of NASA astronauts was formed in 1959. It was part of a program called Project Mercury.

Aldrin with Joan and their children, James Michael (*top left*),
Andrew, and Janice, in the late 1960s

Aldrin joined **NASA** in October 1963. He was part of the third group of astronauts chosen by NASA. Because of his knowledge of **rendezvous** methods, Aldrin's fellow astronauts called him "Dr. Rendezvous."

NASA training was difficult and tiring, but Aldrin enjoyed it. He studied **aerodynamics**, **physics**, astronomy, geology, and more. The astronauts had to prepare for all kinds of emergencies and situations. Aldrin and the other astronauts also underwent survival training in the desert of Nevada and the jungle of Panama. During this training, Aldrin ate **iguana** and **boa constrictor** to survive!

In his early years at NASA, Aldrin created new docking and rendezvous methods. He also came up with underwater training methods to prepare for **space walking**. Aldrin was a frequent **scuba diver**. He recognized that being underwater is much like experiencing **zero gravity**. He practiced moving underwater while wearing a heavy backpack. Other astronauts soon copied Aldrin's methods.

Aldrin practices moving in his spacesuit.

Aldrin was rejected the first time he applied to NASA.
But he was selected when he applied a second time.

6 The Gemini Program

Aldrin's training prepared him for his first big mission. It was part of the Gemini program. Gemini helped **NASA** astronauts improve their skills and practice **space walking**.

Aldrin was the pilot for the *Gemini 12* spacecraft. He was joined by the mission's commander, James Lovell. Aldrin and Lovell launched on November 11, 1966. They spent four days in space.

On the mission, Aldrin set the record for the longest space walk at the time. A space walk is when an astronaut goes outside of a spacecraft. It's called a space walk even though there isn't actually anything to walk on in space. During a space walk, the astronaut is attached to the spacecraft by a cord and floats alongside the spacecraft.

Aldrin's historic space walk lasted five and a half hours. During that time, Aldrin and the *Gemini 12* circled Earth once every 90 minutes. They moved at a speed of 17,500 miles per hour (28,164 kmh)!

STELLAR!

Aldrin took the first selfie in space! He took a photograph of himself on a space walk during the Gemini mission.

Lovell (*second from left*) and Aldrin (*third from left*) are greeted by officers, sailors, and NASA officials aboard the aircraft carrier USS *Wasp*.

Aldrin and Lovell returned to Earth on November 15. This was the last mission in the Gemini program. This program laid the foundation for **NASA's** Apollo missions to the Moon.

Men on the Moon

After the Gemini program, Aldrin worked on the Apollo missions. The goal of the Apollo missions was to put a human on the moon. President John F. Kennedy challenged the United States to do so by the end of the 1960s.

    NASA and its astronauts were determined to meet this goal. Aldrin was chosen to be part of the Apollo 11 mission. He was joined by Neil Armstrong and Michael Collins. Armstrong was the mission commander, while Aldrin was the **lunar module** pilot. Collins would pilot the main spacecraft, *Columbia*.

    Aldrin, Armstrong, and Collins launched into space on July 16, 1969. The astronauts spent two days traveling to the moon. On the third day, they slowed down so the gravity of the moon would draw them into lunar orbit.

    On July 20, Aldrin and Armstrong entered the lunar module, the *Eagle*. The *Eagle* separated from *Columbia*. Aldrin piloted the *Eagle* toward the moon's surface. Aldrin and Armstrong struggled to find a spot to land on the moon. They almost ran out of fuel! They landed with only 15 to 20 seconds of fuel to spare.

Aldrin stands on the moon after setting up scientific equipment near the *Eagle*. Aldrin and Armstrong also planted a US flag on the moon.

Armstrong stepped onto the moon first. Aldrin followed soon after. On the moon, they collected rock samples, conducted experiments, and took photographs. They spent 21 hours on the moon.

Back on the *Eagle*, Aldrin and Armstrong used a second rocket engine to blast off the moon. Their next step was to **rendezvous** with *Columbia*. Aldrin and Armstrong orbited the moon for a few hours, waiting for *Columbia* to come into view. Then, Aldrin guided the *Eagle* to connect with *Columbia*.

Aldrin, Armstrong, and Collins returned to Earth on July 24. Their spacecraft splashed down safely in the Pacific Ocean. The three Apollo 11 astronauts reentered the world as celebrities.

After splashdown, a US Navy Underwater Demolition Team swimmer helped the three astronauts into a life raft. Then they waited to be picked up by a helicopter.

APOLLO ASTRONAUTS

ALAN SHEPARD (1923–1998)

+ First American to go into space, on Mercury-Redstone
+ Commander on Apollo 14, when he became the oldest person to walk on the moon, at age 47

NEIL ARMSTRONG (1930–2012)

+ Command Pilot on Gemini 8, when he became the first person to successfully dock two spacecraft in space
+ Commander on Apollo 11 and the first person to walk on the moon

MICHAEL COLLINS (1930–)

+ Performed a space walk on the Gemini 10 mission
+ Command Module Pilot on Apollo 11

JAMES LOVELL JR. (1928–)

+ Command Module Pilot on Apollo 8, the first mission to orbit the moon
+ Commander on Apollo 13, which was supposed to land on the moon but couldn't due to an explosion on board

Life after NASA

After the moon landing, everyone wanted to know what it was like. The Apollo 11 astronauts began traveling around the world. They gave speeches about the mission to the public, to the US Congress, and to leaders of other nations. These travels continued through 1970.

When he returned home, Aldrin wasn't sure what to do next. He was exhausted from traveling and felt directionless. His marriage to Joan was struggling as well. So, in January 1971, Aldrin announced he was leaving **NASA**.

That summer, Aldrin became commander of the USAF Test Pilot School at Edwards Air Force Base in California. Aldrin struggled at this job. He began to experience **depression** and **alcoholism**. He realized the job was not the right choice and left in 1972.

For several years, Aldrin worked on getting help for his mental health. He also wrote a **memoir**, *Return to Earth*. The book discusses Aldrin's life and mental health issues. *Return to Earth* was published in 1973. A TV movie based on Aldrin's book aired in 1976.

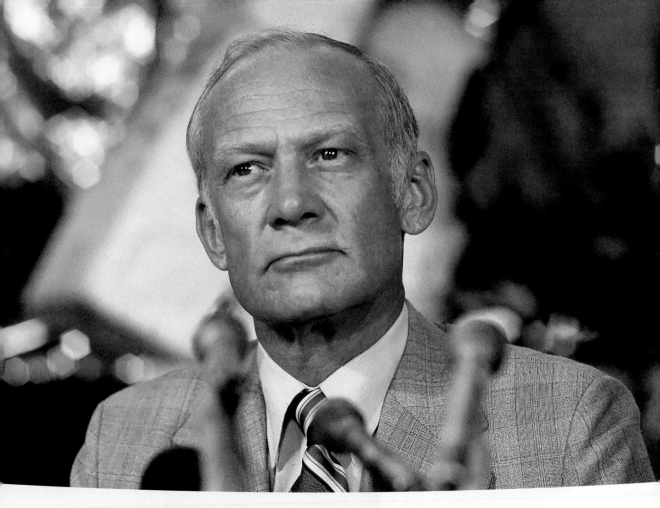

Aldrin frequently speaks about his struggles with mental illness.

Though Aldrin's life began to turn around, his marriage was in trouble. He and Joan divorced in 1974. Soon after, Aldrin met Beverly Van Zile. They were married later that year. However, the marriage didn't last long. The two divorced after a few years.

Buzz the Celebrity

In the 1980s, Aldrin turned his focus back to space. He wanted to make space travel possible for all people, not just astronauts. Aldrin also wanted humans to return to the moon. He thought **NASA** should develop a **lunar** base or space station there. However, Aldrin soon realized Mars would be a better location than the moon.

In 1985, Aldrin developed plans for a spacecraft he called the *Aldrin Mars Cycler*. This spacecraft would be used to transport people to and from a settlement on Mars. He estimated a trip in the *Aldrin Mars Cycler* would take just five months.

That same year, Aldrin met Lois Driggs Cannon. The two soon fell in love and married in 1988. Lois was a huge force in Aldrin's life. She helped Aldrin promote himself and create a business around his celebrity.

In the 1990s, Aldrin started doing interviews and speaking at events across the country. Aldrin found he enjoyed public speaking. He also published several

STELLAR!

Aldrin's ideas for a settlement on Mars are gaining popularity today. Companies such as SpaceX are developing spacecraft to help people travel to and live on other planets.

Aldrin says Lois helped him overcome depression
and brought purpose to his life.

more books. These included *Reaching for the Moon* in 2005 and
Magnificent Desolation: The Long Journey Home from the Moon
in 2009. After years of hardship, Aldrin finally felt like himself
again.

10 Buzz's Legacy

Throughout the years, Aldrin has become a household name. He has guest-starred on many popular TV shows, such as *The Simpsons*, *The Big Bang Theory*, and *30 Rock*. In 2010, he even competed on *Dancing with the Stars* at the age of 80!

Aldrin and Lois divorced in 2012, and he has not married again. Today, Aldrin enjoys spending time with his family. In addition to his three children, he has one grandson and three great-grandsons. Aldrin also continues to travel.

While busy with entertainment and travels, Aldrin hasn't forgotten about space. The Buzz Aldrin Space Institute at the Florida Institute of **Technology** was established in 2015. The institute focuses on sending humans to Mars. Aldrin is a professor and advisor at the institute. He also has patents for a **modular** space station, reusable rockets, and multi-crew modules.

Aldrin had many important accomplishments in **aviation**, space, science, and entertainment. And when faced with challenges, Aldrin never gave up. That's why he remains an inspiration to many people.

Aldrin is still involved in space travel today. He gives speeches on the topic and frequently gives advice to the US government.

Timeline

Edwin "Buzz" Aldrin is born on January 20 in Montclair, New Jersey.

1930

Aldrin flies on 66 missions during the Korean War.

1952–1953

Aldrin goes into space on the Gemini 12 mission.

1966

1951

Aldrin graduates third in his class from West Point.

1963

Aldrin is accepted to NASA after applying for a secor time. He is part of the third group of astronauts.

Aldrin, Armstrong, and Collins go on the Apollo 11 mission to the moon and back. Armstrong and Aldrin are the first humans to walk on the moon.

1969

Aldrin develops the *Aldrin Mars Cycler* to travel between Earth and Mars.

1985

1971

Aldrin leaves NASA.

1973

Return to Earth, Aldrin's first book, is published.

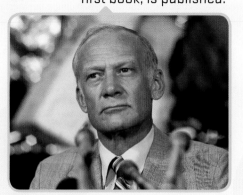

2015

The Buzz Aldrin Space Institute is established at the Florida Institute of Technology.

Glossary

aerodynamics—the science of what qualities make an object move easily and quickly through air.

alcoholism—a disorder in which a person cannot control his or her urge to drink alcohol.

American Revolution—from 1775 to 1783. A war for independence between Great Britain and its North American colonies. The colonists won and created the United States of America.

astronautics—the science of building and operating spacecraft.

aviation—the operation and navigation of aircraft.

boa constrictor—a large snake that kills its prey by squeezing it with its body.

cadet—a student in a military school.

chaplain—a religious leader that works in a branch of the military.

depression—a state of feeling sad or dejected.

iguana—a large tropical lizard that has a line of tall scales along its back.

integrity—the state or act of being honest and sincere.

Korean War—a war fought in North and South Korea from 1950 to 1953. The US government sent troops to help South Korea.

lunar—of or relating to the moon.

memoir (MEHM-wahr)—a written account of a person's experiences.

module—a self-contained, independent part of a spacecraft having a specific function. Something built with modules is modular.

NASA—National Aeronautics and Space Administration. NASA is a US government agency that manages the nation's space program and conducts flight research.

PhD—doctor of philosophy. Usually, this is the highest degree a student can earn.

physics—a science that studies matter and energy and how they interact.

rendezvous—the process of bringing two spacecraft together.

scuba diver—a person who uses scuba gear while swimming underwater. Scuba gear allows people to breathe underwater.

space walk—an activity in which an astronaut does work outside a spacecraft while it is in space.

technology (tehk-NAH-luh-jee)—machinery and equipment developed for practical purposes using scientific principles and engineering.

zero gravity—the absence of weight, as in outer space.

ONLINE RESOURCES

Booklinks
NONFICTION
NETWORK
FREE! ONLINE NONFICTION RESOURCES

To learn more about Buzz Aldrin, visit **abdobooklinks.com**. These links are routinely monitored and updated to provide the most current information available.

Index